STRUGGLE FOR SURVIV

Fire

Christine Dugan, M.A.Ed.

Consultants

Timothy Rasinski, Ph.D.
Kent State University

Lori Oczkus, M.A.
Literacy Consultant

Christopher Nyerges
Author and Educator;
Cofounder of School of Self-Reliance

Publishing Credits

Rachelle Cracchiolo, M.S.Ed., *Publisher*
Conni Medina, M.A.Ed., *Managing Editor*
Dona Herweck Rice, *Series Developer*
Emily R. Smith, M.A.Ed., *Content Director*
Stephanie Bernard and Seth Rogers, *Editors*
Robin Erickson, *Multimedia Designer*

The TIME logo is a registered trademark of TIME Inc. Used under license.

Image Credits: p.6 Verdateo/Dreamstime.com; pp.6-7 Rvc5pogod/
Dreamstime.com; pp.12-13 Daitoiumihai/Dreamstime.com; pp.14-15,
19 Illustrations by Kevin Pham; pp.34-35 Jerry Schad/Science Source;
p.39 David Vaughan/Science Source; pp.40-41 Stephen J. Krasemann/
Science Source; pp.42-43 William Attard Mccarthy/Dreamstime.com;
pp.44-45 Zoya Fedorova/Dreamstime.com; all other images from
iStock and/or Shutterstock.

Notes: Care and caution should always be practiced when using
tools and methods for survival. The answers to the mathematics
problems posed throughout the book are provided on page 48.

Teacher Created Materials
5301 Oceanus Drive
Huntington Beach, CA 92649-1030
http://www.tcmpub.com
ISBN 978-1-4938-3605-5

Table of Contents

In a Cold, Dark World 4

The Importance of Fire for Survival . . . 6

Starting a Fire. 14

The Lights Are Out in the City 22

In the Woods 30

Deserted in the Desert 36

Survival of the Fittest 42

Glossary 44

Index 45

Check It Out! 46

Try It! 47

About the Author 48

In a Cold, Dark World

What do you think it would be like to suddenly have the world go dark? All the modern inventions you expect to easily use—lights, cell phones, computers—suddenly stop working. It is hard to imagine such an extreme situation as being somewhere with no phone, no electricity, and no Internet.

Consider what you might need to survive such a scenario. It is always good to be prepared for anything that could happen. If the world suddenly goes dark for a long period of time, you may start looking for the basic necessities to survive. Heat and light are important for survival, but where would you find heat and light in an emergency?

The skills needed to survive a serious emergency do not require heroic acts or great physical strength. The skills you need to stay alive will work if you keep calm and make good choices. You need to know about the environment you are in when disaster strikes. How can that environment help you? What challenges do you need to overcome? Facing a tough situation with determination will help you stay alive!

Trying It Out

You can take a survival class and practice different ways to stay alive. The Boulder Outdoor Survival School claims to be the oldest survival school in the world. You can learn how to make rope, start a fire, build a shelter, and identify **edible** plants.

Practice Carefully!

To be prepared for a disaster, you may want to practice some of the fire-starting suggestions in this book. Always make sure an adult is present to help, and only practice under safe conditions! Fire is not a toy and must be respected.

The Importance of Fire for Survival

Imagine the planet in total darkness. It might feel like being transported back in time. What was it like when people had to survive off the land with only the most primitive resources? What did people use as sources of heat and light?

Fire, one of the most important forces of nature, is a truly valued resource. But be careful—it can have both positive and negative impacts since fire can both help and harm you. Fire provides heat and light, which is necessary to **sustain** and regenerate life. But it can also be very destructive and can damage anything in its path in the blink of an eye.

Fire has been a key part of survival for millions of years. If you are building a fire to survive, you probably want the fire to provide many different things. You'll need fire to stay warm and dry, especially in cold areas, which is essential for survival. Fire can also **illuminate** the darkness, and having fire means you can cook food or melt snow or ice into drinking water. Smoke from a fire could also help others locate you.

1400°C

1200°C

1000°C

800°C

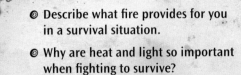

THINK LINK

- Describe what fire provides for you in a survival situation.
- Why are heat and light so important when fighting to survive?
- Which do you think is more important: heat or light?

How Hot Is That Flame?

You know fire is hot, but how hot is it? That depends on the type of fire and the environment in which it is burning. Even a candle has different temperatures within it. Look at the diagram and determine the difference between the hottest and coldest part of the candle flame.

What Is Fire?

Fire is a chemical reaction between oxygen and some type of fuel, such as wood. This is also called **combustion**. Here is what happens when wood is heated and catches fire.

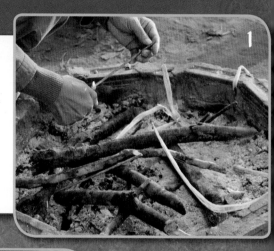

Watch It Ignite!

Something has to ignite the wood, which means something heats the wood to a temperature at which a fire begins. The heat can come from a source such as a match, lightning, friction, or focused light.

Up in Smoke

The wood reaches about 302 degrees Fahrenheit (°F), which is the same as 150 degrees Celsius (°C). The wood starts breaking down because of the heat, so part of the wood is changing from a solid into a gas. The gas is in the smoke that starts to rise.

Flaming Fire

The wood continues to burn and turns into *char*, which is made up of **carbon** and ash. This creates the flames that rise from the fire. These flames can be different colors depending on the fuel that is burning and how hot the fire is.

Putting It Out

When it's time to put out the fire, the fuel (wood), the heat, or the oxygen must be removed. Taking wood out of a fire can be very tricky when the wood is hot. The most common (and safest) methods are to remove the heat from fire by **dousing** it with water or to remove the oxygen by **smothering** the fire with dirt or sand.

Staying Warm

You can't survive in cold environments for long without proper clothing and shelter. Without heat or protection, you risk letting your body temperature drop too low. Heat sources help keep your body warm and dry. With proper heat, you can survive cold temperatures and wet surroundings.

Cover Those Hands and Feet!

Some body parts often cool faster than your body's core. They include feet, hands, nose, and ears. This is why it is important to keep them covered and protected.

Body Temperatures

Hypothermia occurs when your body temperature is dangerously low (below 95°F or 35°C) from cold temperature or **exposure**. A healthy core body temperature is between 98°F and 99°F (36.7°C and 37.2°C).

Here are the conversions for changing Fahrenheit to Celsius and Celsius to Fahrenheit.

- ◎ To convert F to C: subtract 32, multiply by 5, and divide by 9.
- ◎ To covert C to F: multiply by 9, divide by 5, and add 32.

If your body temperature is 92°F, what is it in °C?

If your body temperature is 37°C, what is it in °F?

The Perfect Temperature

You are always trying to find the right temperature that feels good for your body. Usually when you feel cold, you can turn up the heat in your house or car. Your family might build a fire in a fireplace using matches, newspaper, and wood. Or maybe they simply ignite the gas. You can cuddle under blankets or layer on extra clothes. But if you need to stay warm and dry to survive in an emergency situation, you must know how to light a fire or generate heat in different ways.

Can You Overdo It in the Cold?

The main purpose of building a fire in an emergency is to keep you warm. Creating a warm fire, covering your body with proper clothing, and building a shelter will all help you stay warm.

Moving and keeping your body active will also help you stay warm. Movement keeps your body's blood circulating, which moves heat throughout your body to places such as your fingers and toes.

Sweating in the Snow

If you work too hard and start sweating in the cold, you might develop a problem. The sweat can freeze next to your skin, drawing away heat from your body. The sweat can also make your clothing wet, reducing its ability to keep you warm.

But is there a way you can overdo it? Can you cause other problems by moving too much? Most certainly! Movement and activity cause your body to burn calories. Your body needs those calories to stay warm. As your body burns its necessary calories, it is easier for hypothermia to set in.

Wear Your Layers

Experts say that the best way to dress for the cold is to dress in layers. You need a base layer to keep moisture off your body, a middle layer that traps heat, and a top layer to protect you from the cold and wind.

Starting a Fire

In a perfect world, you would be able to create a fire in a flat area without any wind. There would also be a large supply of wood nearby, and you could start a fire simply by building the perfect structure and igniting it with the flick of a single match. But how could you do that in the pouring rain or in the middle of a city or a desert? What if you had no matches or lighters, and you didn't have any pieces of dry wood? You may have to get creative about how and where you start a fire, but luckily, there are many ways to get flames going!

The Dakota Fire Hole

Building a fire hole helps you burn fuel more efficiently and use less wood. American Indians developed this special method to create fire in windy areas such as the Dakotas in the Great Plains.

Heat and smoke escape through the hole above the fire, which stops air from coming down into the hole.

A decreased airflow means that the fire will burn fuel slower than if it were started above ground.

Location, Location, Location

Some places are more ideal for building fires and keeping them going than others. Try to find dry ground and a flat surface. You want your fire to be close to a source of wood and close to your sources of shelter and water. Once you've found a good spot, you're ready to light the fire.

Begin by gathering wood and stacking it in a tepee-like shape in your selected fire area. The wood should be dry and positioned so that it can easily catch and maintain fire. The tepee shape will help the fire burn steadily without being smothered. Once your wood stack is ready, you can begin to light the fire.

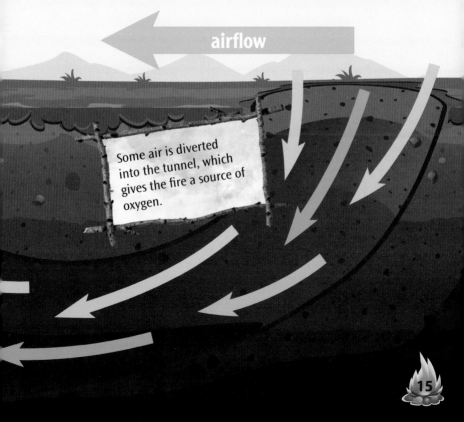

airflow

Some air is diverted into the tunnel, which gives the fire a source of oxygen.

It Only Takes a Spark

Tinder, kindling, and logs are different types of fuel necessary to start fires. Tinder is the light material that catches fire easily with one spark. This might be grass, leaves, moss, or straw that is completely dry. Usually, a pile of tinder that is about the size of two fists is enough to get a fire started.

From Tinder to Flame

Lighting tinder is the first step in getting a fire going, and it only takes a single spark! Matches allow you to do this quickly, but if disaster strikes and you don't have any matches available, you will need to rely on other materials. Rubbing two pieces of wood together can create enough heat to start a spark. **Flint** is a kind of metal that will produce sparks when steel is rubbed against it. A magnifying glass or a camera lens lined up with the sun can create a hot spot that will ignite tinder.

At first, it might seem impossible to start even the smallest spark. Be patient, and don't give up. Remember that people have been starting fires for a million years. With the right materials and a persistent attitude, you can get a fire going, too.

Fire Tools

Starting a fire is much easier with the proper tools. An axe or a knife is essential for fire making because you can cut wood into smaller pieces. These tools can also be used to split wood to get the dry parts from inside a log. If you don't have an axe or a knife, you can make one using a sharp stone and a wooden handle.

Clear the Area

Don't build a fire where it is unsafe or where other objects may catch fire. Find a spot away from dry trees and brush. Consider how strong the wind is blowing when building a fire. Remember that a forest fire would be a much bigger problem for you to solve!

17

A Bow Drill

What happens when you don't have matches handy? Don't worry; there are ways to meet this extreme challenge! One method of fire starting has been used for thousands of years and is called the *bow drill*, which consists of a fire board, a bow, a drill or a spindle, and a socket or a "handhold."

The fire board consists of a soft, dry wooden board. The preliminary step includes digging out part of the center of the board to make a small pit. Cut a notch in the fire board from the pit to the edge. Once you've completed these steps, place the board on the ground so the notch is directly above a small pile of tinder.

Next, construct a bow by curving a branch and tying a string or a rope to each end. Twist the drill around the bow's string, and situate the drill in the small pit. The socket, which should be made of hard wood, goes above the drill and is where you will apply pressure to hold the drill in place.

Responsibility with Fire

Whether you're lighting a match or building a fire for survival, it is always important to use extreme caution. Even a small fire can get out of control quickly.

Once you have the bow, drill, and socket prepared, you're ready to start your fire. If there is any discernable wind, try to position yourself so that your body creates a blockade from the wind to prevent it from blowing out your fire. Firmly press down on the socket with one hand and quickly pull the bow back and forth with the other, thus spinning the drill. The friction against the fire board will create smoke, which will slowly become a small **ember**. Gently blowing on the ember will produce a fire! This method takes time and effort, so remember to be patient and persistent.

A Matchbook, Please!

Today, matches make it easy to start fires. Matchbooks were invented in the late 1800s. Match heads contain sulfur that ignites and sets the matchstick on fire.

19

A Toothpaste Fire?

If only you could start a fire with familiar items you might have in your home . . . . Well, you can! You can start a fire with an **aluminum** soda can and toothpaste. Getting innovative about how to make flames may help you survive **dire** situations. This trick requires sunlight and tinder.

The bottoms of soda cans often have dull finishes. If you look closely at a can, you'll see there are subtle lines that indicate the grain of the aluminum. These lines make it difficult for the sun's rays to reflect off the can because the lines scatter the rays. A polished can bottom that looks like a mirror works better for reflecting and concentrating sunlight.

Fire Starters

Fire starters are good to add to an emergency kit. They can be useful when you have no tinder to burn or when you want to create fires quickly. You can buy fire starters or make your own. With an adult's help, place dryer lint in an egg carton. Then melt wax and pour that onto the cups, covering the lint. Once the wax dries, cut apart the cups. These small fire starters make small but useful flames that will burn for about 10 minutes. That's enough time for the bigger pieces of wood in your fire to catch.

To get started on a toothpaste fire, rub toothpaste on the bottom of the can in tiny circles. You're actually using the toothpaste to polish the can. Wipe off the excess toothpaste. If you do it well, the bottom of the can should clearly reflect your face as you look at it.

Then, place some tinder at the center of the can bottom. Point the bottom of the can toward the sun, and eventually the tinder should start to **smolder** as the sun's rays reflect off the bottom of the can. Once the tinder is smoldering, add it to a bigger bundle and blow until a flame appears.

Soda Can Angle

When polishing the bottom of the can, you make an average of 150 circles on the can per minute. It takes you 14 minutes 30 seconds to get the can fully polished. How many circles would you have made?

value

toothpaste

Quality Guaranteed

The Lights Are Out in the City

If you are ever trapped in a cold, dark place with no easy way to make light and heat, stay calm. Remember, there are several different things you can do to stay alive and safe. What you need to do to survive depends on where you are and what materials you have available. If you are in a city, what could you use for heat and light to stay alive?

Help From FEMA

FEMA stands for the Federal Emergency Management Agency. This is the government office that helps cities and states in the United States deal with natural disasters.

Safety First

Many experts advise leaving the city as soon as possible in the event of a **catastrophe**. There might be more resources available to you in a city at first, but there would also be more people looking for those same materials. Soon, people may fight over food and water. That kind of conflict can become dangerous.

A Lightbulb Moment

Modern inventions help us create light with the flip of a switch. What an unsettling idea to think of a disaster in which lamps and lightbulbs would not work. Here is a list of important light inventions:

- 1780—oil lamp
- 1792—gas lamp
- 1867—fluorescent lamp
- 1875—electric lightbulb
- 1962—light-emitting diode (LED) lights

How many years ago were LED lights invented?

Bug-Out Pack

In the event of a serious emergency, some city **dwellers** may want to get out of the cities as quickly as possible. This means planning ahead and being prepared and packed are key. Getting together a "bug-out pack" is part of this plan.

This special pack includes a large backpack filled with essential items. These items would allow you to survive for a long time away from cities. It is not the same as an emergency kit. This is something you would likely wear on your back and travel with for long distances. You'll want to pack carefully and strategically, so you have everything you need.

Points on a Compass

There are four cardinal points on a compass—North, South, East, and West. There are intercardinal points (NE, SE, SW, NW) and secondary intercardinal points (NNW, NNE, ENE, ESE, SSE, SSW, WSW, WNW) as well.

Inside the Pack

These are some essential items you may find in a bug-out pack:

- water and filters
- nonperishable food for at least three days
- two sets of clothes so you have one that is dry at all times
- tent and sleeping bag
- first aid kit
- fire starters
- rope or cord
- multi-tool, including a knife
- solar recharger
- compass
- lighting tool (headlamp, candle, or LED light)

Finding Your Way

If you are familiar with where you are in the woods, you might want to know how to find your way to other landmarks. A compass is an important tool to help you navigate your direction and location in the woods.

Be Prepared: Creating an Emergency Fire-Making Kit

One of the best ways to help survive a situation without lights or heat is to have an emergency fire-making kit. You can gather supplies and store them safely. This means you'll know where to find essential items if you ever need them. Having an emergency kit requires thinking and planning. You may never need it, but it's a good thing to have just in case.

People often think about storing food and medical supplies first, but other common items are also important to have, especially for fire making. If you have access to a kit like this, you will be more likely to create the fire needed to survive.

- **Save a Light**—To stay warm and dry, the first thing you'll need in your kit is a variety of lighting tools. Waterproof and windproof matches are best. So is a lighter. Flint tools are great things to add to your kit, too.

- **Where's the Rope?**—Superfine steel wool and a short rope are good to have in your kit. Both things can be used as tinder. And the rope may also be helpful in building a shelter.

- ◎ **Magnify the Problem**—A magnifying glass is also useful. This can be used with the sun to create hot spots to light tinder.

- ◎ **Lip Balm Fire?**—Add a tube of petroleum-jelly lip balm to your kit. So you won't have chapped lips? No! You can use it on your tinder to make it burn hotter and longer.

- ◎ **Warm Blanket**—Don't forget a thermal blanket. These blankets are lightweightand should not take up much space, but they keep you warm and help prevent hypothermia. Even if you build a fire for warmth, a thermal blanket is essential.

Afraid of the Dark?

It's difficult to imagine a large populated city going completely dark. But it has happened, and it will probably happen again. It pays to be prepared and know how to create light from different resources. While knowing how to build a fire for light is a great skill, you only want to do that if you absolutely have to. Prepare ahead of time by gathering things that already make light (such as flashlights, lanterns, and candles) in an emergency kit.

Knowing what common items can be used as sources of light is an important survival skill. Did you know that crayons make excellent candles? These colored tubes of wax will burn for about 30 minutes each. If something happens to your candles or flashlights, crayons can be great last-minute replacements.

A large fire, or bonfire, can help you stay warm and create ample light. But you should be very careful where you build any fires. Make sure all fires are located in safe places and that they won't spread out of control. Ideally, you would have some tools on hand for cutting firewood. A chainsaw would be great, but it requires fuel, so you might need to locate smaller tools, such as an axe or a log splitter.

Bonfire 101

There is a science to building a bonfire. The tepee, or pyramid shape, usually suggested helps create a chimney effect. This shape also increases the intensity of the fire.

Volume of a Pyramid Fire

If a fire is built as a pyramid with a rectangular base, you can determine the volume of the pyramid.

$$V = \frac{lwh}{3}$$

If the fire pyramid is 1.2 feet long, 2.2 feet wide, and 3.4 feet high, what is the volume of the pyramid?

In the Woods

You may think that trying to survive in a city is a challenge. However, staying alive in the woods can be extremely difficult. It's worse if you don't have proper supplies or modern conveniences, such as matches, flashlights, and fuel, to help make survival easier. Two important factors to be mindful of in the woods are the time of year and the weather conditions. For example, a wooded environment in winter may have dangerously low temperatures.

One main goal for survival in a wooded area is to stay warm and dry. A fire will help with that goal. But you also need proper clothing to protect your body and keep it heated. Wearing a hat is key because more than 40 percent of your body heat is lost through the top of your head.

Chilly Wind

Surviving the cold means being aware of things such as **windchill**. This means how cold the air feels on your skin.

Windchill Chart

Wind Speed	Equivalent Temperature (°F)				
0 MPH	40°	20°	0°	−20°	−40°
10 MPH	28°	4°	−21°	−46°	−70°
20 MPH	18°	−10°	−39°	−67°	−96°
30 MPH	13°	−18°	−48°	−79°	−109°
40 MPH	10°	−21°	−53°	−85°	−116°

STOP! THINK...

◎ If the temperature is −20°F outside and the wind is approximately 10 MPH, how cold will the air feel?

◎ If the temperature is 20°F outside, what speed wind will lower the temperature you feel to −18°F?

◎ If the temperature is 40°F outside but the wind is approximately 30 MPH, how much colder will the air feel?

Lighting Up the Forest

For thousands of years, pine knot torches have illuminated the darkest places on Earth. A pine knot is the dead bark inside a pine tree, and it makes a remarkable light for people to carry and use in the woods. Knowing how to make a torch from this part of a tree is a useful skill for all survivalists.

There are necessary tools, such as hatchets or saws, that are required to complete this project. Securing a hatchet or saw will simplify your task, but a small knife will be sufficient to get the job done. Figure out which tool can be used to light the torch and keep it burning successfully.

Keep It Lit

Imagine you are surviving in the woods and you make a torch to last each night for five nights in a row. Using the information below, what is the average amount of time the torch provided light?

Night 1: 4 hours 32 minutes

Night 2: 4 hours 54 minutes

Night 3: 3 hours 5 minutes

Night 4: 5 hours 17 minutes

Night 5: 4 hours 44 minutes

32

Here are the steps for making a pine knot torch:

- Find a dead pine tree limb and rip off the bark.

- Gather the bark from the tree, and tie it together with string or rope. You can also split the knot end of the limb into four sections and then stuff twigs and wood shavings into those sections.

- Light the end of the torch, and watch it burn for several hours!

Light the Way

Torches are the most basic kinds of flashlights and have been used for thousands of years. Holding a light in a dark place not only helps you see your surroundings better but also helps you see where to step to prevent tripping and injuring yourself.

Look Up for Light

Even if the woods are incredibly dark, there might be one thing in nature to light the way—the night sky. The night sky not only provides some natural light, but it also provides information about the general direction in which you are moving.

The moon moves from east to west as it crosses the sky. In the Northern Hemisphere, the sunlit part of the moon appears to move from right to left. In the Southern Hemisphere, the sunlit part the moon appears to move from left to right.

The glow of the daytime sun can provide not only heat and light but also a reference for direction. The sun follows a constant path as it rises in the east and sets in the west. So, pay close attention to the direction in which the sun is moving.

Stars and constellations can be helpful, too. The constellation Orion rises in the east and sets in the west, matching the path of the sun. Finding the North Star will allow you to position yourself facing north. All you have to do is imagine a line down to the horizon from the North Star.

Phases of the Moon

If you look up at the night sky, the moon will look different depending on which phase it is in. The moon has eight phases:

first quarter

waxing gibbous

waxing crescent

full moon

new moon

waning gibbous

waning crescent

third quarter

Fractions of the Moon

As the moon cycles through its phases, different fractions become visible.

Approximately what fraction of the moon shows during the waning gibbous phase?

Which two moon phases represent $\frac{1}{2}$?

Which moon phases are closest to $\frac{1}{8}$?

35

Deserted in the Desert

When disaster strikes, it often happens quickly and without warning. You don't always have time to prepare or to get to the most comfortable environment. What would survival techniques look like if you were stuck in the desert without an easy way to create heat or light?

It may seem as if a desert would be an ideal place for heat and light. It's so hot and sunny there, so why would you need to worry about staying warm? Well, deserts have extreme temperatures. The climate can be

Too Hot and Too Cold

Desert temperatures can be above 120°F (48.9 °C) during summer days, but they can also go far below freezing in wintertime, even to −0.4°F (−18°C)!

very hot, but it can also be extremely cold. A desert's climate determines whether it is a cold desert or a hot desert. A hot desert is a dry environment with little rain or snow. It is often hot during the day but can get quite cold at night. A cold desert gets more rain and snow but is also a dry environment that has extremely cold temperatures.

Dry Land

A desert is a dry area that receives very little precipitation, usually less than 10 inches (25.4 centimeters) per year. Precipitation in a hot desert typically refers to rain, while cold deserts receive snow.

Surviving the Cold

Most people don't live in cold deserts, so it is unlikely that you would need to prepare to survive in a cold desert. But it could happen. What is more likely, though, is a situation in which you would be in a hot desert at night or in the winter months. You would need very specific and advanced survival skills to handle the cold temperatures and darkness in such a **desolate** place.

Your main goal in cold climates is to stay warm, but it's easy to panic and feel overwhelmed when you are in harsh environments. Remember that an important aspect of survival is the ability to stay calm. Think about what you need to survive each situation you face. Look at the resources available to you. Consider how you might build a fire to stay warm in an area with few trees or plants.

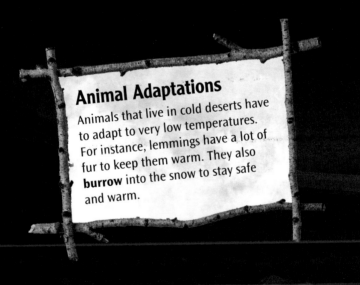

Animal Adaptations

Animals that live in cold deserts have to adapt to very low temperatures. For instance, lemmings have a lot of fur to keep them warm. They also **burrow** into the snow to stay safe and warm.

Antarctica Population

Many scientists live and work in Antarctica, which has the world's largest cold desert. There are about 4,000 people there in the summer months, but fewer people stay for the harsh winters.

Desert Dilemma

Building a fire in cities or in the woods may be easier than in a desert because there are more things available to burn. A desert environment has very few trees or bushes. With that in mind, how can you create a fire in the desert so you'll have heat and light to stay warm and safe?

Fire Protection

Building a fire in a survival situation can do more than give heat and light. It also adds a layer of protection from dangerous animals, including snakes and scorpions.

black scorpion

yucca plant

Know Your Plants

You have to make smart decisions in the desert about what you burn. It's good to know which of the desert plants are the most effective for burning warm fires. Yucca and juniper plants are two of the best fire-starting plants. Yucca plants have dry flower stalks that make good material for fires. Juniper plants are helpful because they provide wood and fiber that burn easily.

Clean Up While You Warm Up

Yucca plants have leaves that make great soap. Native tribes in the American Southwest discovered this long ago. Who knew you could stay clean using plants?!

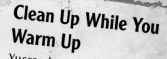

THINK LINK

- Describe the progression of a fire from the moment it starts until it is extinguished.

- How can you start a fire without a match?

- What can happen if you are exposed to extreme cold?

Survival of the Fittest

Staying calm in tough situations is always an important first step. If you find yourself in an emergency and you have to think about ways to find heat and light, consider what you already know. Where are you, and what can your environment provide to keep you warm? What objects can help you make light so you can see where you are and where you want to go? What would be the easiest and safest way to build a fire?

Survival skills have improved over the last thousand years. Today, you may not have to use those skills often, but if you ever do, you are certainly capable of successfully completing the necessary tasks to find heat and light. Trust yourself, and look to your surroundings to help you find your way to safety.

Believe in Yourself

Winston Churchill, the one-time prime minster of England, once said, "Never, never, never give up." To know that you are going to survive a challenging situation, you have to believe in yourself and not give up.

Surviving on TV

Survival skills are so important that they have made television shows about them! The television show *Survivor* is shown in many countries. It involves watching people being stranded in remote places and having to survive.

Glossary

aluminum—a metal found in the earth's crust

burrow—to hide by digging an underground hole

carbon—a chemical element that forms coal

catastrophe—a sudden disaster

combustion—the act of burning

desolate—lonely or abandoned

dire—extreme

dousing—putting out a fire with water

dwellers—people who live in certain places

edible—safe to eat

ember—a glowing piece of wood from a fire

exposure—to be without shelter or protection

flint—a hard mineral that produces a spark when struck by steel

hypothermia—the reduction of body temperature to a low level

illuminate—to light up

kindling—a material that burns easily and is used to start a fire

smolder—to burn slowly without flames

smothering—covering a fire to put it out

sustain—to keep going

tinder—a light material that burns easily

windchill—the temperature your body feels when air is combined with wind

Index

Antarctica, 39

bonfire, 28

Boulder Outdoor Survival School, 5

bow drill, 18

bug-out pack, 24–25

Churchill, Winston, 43

compass, 24–25

constellations, 34

Dakota Fire Hole, 14

desert, cold and hot, 14, 36–41

emergency kit, 20, 24, 26, 28

FEMA, 22

fire starters, 20, 25

fire temperature, 7–8

fire tools, 17

flint, 16, 26

hypothermia, 11, 13, 27

North Star, 34

Orion, 34

phases of the moon, 35

pine knot torch, 32–33

Survivor, 43

windchill, 30–31

Check It Out!

Books

George, Jean Craighead. 2004. *My Side of the Mountain*. Puffin Books.

_____. 2009. *Pocket Guide to the Outdoors*. Dutton Children's Books.

Levy, Joel. 2012. *How to Be a World Explorer: Your All-Terrain Training Manual*. Weldon Owen Publishing.

McNab, Chris. 2008. *The Boy's Book of Outdoor Survival: 101 Courageous Skills for Exploring the Dangerous Wild*. Ulysses Press.

Nyerges, Christopher. 2014. *How to Survive Anywhere: A Guide for Urban, Suburban, Rural, and Wilderness Environments*. Stackpole Books.

O'Dell, Scott. 2010. *Island of the Blue Dolphins*. HMH Books for Young Readers.

Paulsen, Gary. 2006. *Hatchet*. Simon & Schuster Books for Young Readers.

Websites

Nyerges, Christopher. *School of Self-Reliance*. http://www.christophernyerges.com/.

Practical Survivor. *Starting a Fire in Adverse Weather*. http://www.practicalsurvivor.com/fireintherain

Wild Backpacker. *How to Build a Fire*. http://www.wildbackpacker.com/wilderness-survival/articles/how-to-build-a-fire/